How to Write a Blog, How to Make Money from Blogging

Tips to help you Confront Your Finances, Reduce Your Expenses and Increase Your Income

Richard G Lowe, Jr

How to Write a Blog, How to Make Money from Blogging

Insider Secrets from a Professional Blogger Proven Tips and tricks Every Blogger Needs to Know to Make Money

Professional Freelance Writer Series #2

Published by The Writing King
www.thewritingking.com

How to Write a Blog, How to Make Money from Blogging

Cover Artist: theamateurzone

ASIN: B012GB5QXG
ISBN: 978-1-943517-75-6 (Hardcover)
ISBN: 978-1-943517-74-9 (Paperback)
ISBN: 978-1-943517-09-1 (eBook)

Table of Contents

Introduction

There is an art to writing an article that prompts the reader to make a decision to do something. That's the narrow focus of the book that you are reading on your eBook right now. You will learn how to create an article that gets a reader interested, entices them, informs them, and causes them to make a decision by the time they are finished.

I have a long history in writing articles for the web. I've written papers and technical documents since the beginning of my career. Generally these were dry, formal, highly technical tomes serving a very narrow purpose of informing somebody how to use or support an application. About six years after I was married, my life changed. I found myself needing to write.

In the year 2010, my wife was very ill. My life revolved around her and my job. In order to remain sane, I had to find an outlet. I started up a few websites and began writing articles. I wrote over thousand articles on every conceivable subject. I would pump out one or two every day. Half of them concerned technical subjects relating to computers or the Internet. The rest were a random mishmash of whatever was on my mind at the time.

I posted these articles on my websites and created the HTML code for each one using Notepad. In fact, all of my websites—totaling at least several thousand pages—were hand-coded. In today's age of applications like WordPress, you couldn't even imagine the amount of effort that I put into writing and maintaining those sites.

Introduction

In 2013, I decided it was time to take an early retirement from my very well-paying job with Trader Joe's and accomplish some personal goals. I moved from California to Florida, took some classes, and settled in to work towards achieving them. One of my biggest objectives was to start up a writing career.

I've loved writing since I was a child, which is probably why I took it up as a hobby while my wife was ill. I have the ability to write very quickly; generally, I can produce 10,000 words per day.

As I began to establish myself as a writer, I was faced with one question: what do I write? After some thought and a couple of false starts, I settled on four different career thrusts, which were:

- To produce short, informative eBooks on a wide variety of subjects
- To complete the novels I have been working on for years
- To ghostwrite books for people
- To blog like a madman

As it happens, ghostwriting has turned out to be very lucrative. I seem to have a knack for taking ideas from a person's mind—or, as I like to call it, their mental Post-It Notes—and create a coherent story. I enjoy ghostwriting and have written another book this series describing my technique.

However, the problem with ghostwriting is that for every hour you put in, you get paid for an hour of work. That's the typical conundrum faced by every contractor or consultant: one hour of work equals one hour of pay.

This is why the other three things on my list are designed to produce products that, assuming they are marketed correctly, continue to make money over time. The short e-books sell very well and retain their value over time. Presumably, the novels will work the same way. While a lot more effort goes into writing a novel versus a short eBooks, writing novels is probably the thing that I enjoy the most about my new career.

Blogs, on the other hand, serve two purposes. First, I can work as a consultant and sell my blogging services. Second, part of being an author these days is to produce content all over the Internet. Much of that content is intended to entice people to purchase my books.

There are, of course, several different kinds of blogs. There are those that people write for their own enjoyment and to educate others. These were the kind of blogs I wrote when my wife was ill. They're not designed to make money, although they can; they're more of a hobby.

Some blogs are intended to provide information about a company, product, or person. These don't directly sell a product or service. Instead, they are subtly promoting a concept, idea, person, or company.

The third type of blog is what will be talking about in this book. These contain articles that are designed to directly create income. This involves a skill called copywriting, which is a very specialized talent.

Copywriting is what most people think of as marketing or advertising. I'm sure you've received letters in the mail or email that attempt to get you to purchase something. Better

Introduction

written and professional advertising copy may actually succeed in that goal.

Let me give you an example from my own experience. I received an email offering training to produce short e-books. This was from a company called Author Audience Academy. The email was designed to pull me in so that I would read the text. The first few paragraphs generated an emotion of excitement to keep me reading. The remainder of the email informed me about the program. By the end, the message was loud and clear: I needed to press the buy button and purchase the course. It was one of the best purchases that I've made in my life, as it provided training on how to create and market short e-books from beginning to end.

The book you are reading now describes the method I use to create blog articles specifically intended to work a person from the time they click the link until they push the buy or subscribe button at the bottom of the page. Everything described is specific to that type of writing. Other forms of blogs use different styles; I will address those in future volumes in this series.

I'm not going to get into the psychology of why this works, or what makes people buy things. The purpose here is to describe the mechanics of writing an article that causes someone make a decision—preferably the one that I want them to make.

This type of article can be one of the more difficult forms to write. You cannot just bang them out in an hour two. You'll begin by determining your purpose and writing an outline.

Then, you will write and revise half a dozen times, add pictures, add some videos, and even test it to see if it works the way you think it will work.

Yes, writing this kind of article will take up a large chunk of your time. However, when you consider that a well-written blog article can generate an amount of sales limited only by the number of people you can get to read it, it's time well spent.

I don't claim to know everything there is to know about copywriting. What I am describing in this book is a mixture of techniques that I learned over the last few years. There are many courses offered by various organizations that can provide in-depth and detailed training on the subject. This book, I hope, can start you in the right direction.

I hope you enjoy what I've written and find it to be of some value. If you would like to send me a note about this book, feel free to write me at rich@thewritingking.com. If you enjoyed the book, please write a positive review.

Before you start

Many blog articles are written to promote a service or product. This is a specific form of writing known as copywriting. The general public refers to it as advertising or marketing. The purpose of copywriting is to get someone to do something.

That is the entire purpose put succinctly: to cause someone to take action or to make a decision. Of course, you also present information, make arguments, address objections, and even educate your readers. However, the reason you do all this is so that they make a decision to do something and then do it.

In political advertising, the goal is to sway a person's vote towards a particular candidate. To do this, your article might focus on the candidate's strengths and why he or she is the best for the job. Alternately, the article might focus on the reasons other candidates are corrupt, stupid, or lacking the leadership needed for that position.

I recently wrote a blog article about flood insurance. It turns out that most people routinely purchase this type of insurance because FEMA tells them it is required. However, there's a good likelihood they can get this requirement removed if they reside in an area that has little to no risk of a flood.

In this case, I began by asking readers if they enjoyed paying for something they didn't need. Could they use an extra thousand dollars a year for something else? Did they know they might be wasting that much money year after year? After that, I provided information on the subject, and by the time the reader had finished, the article the choice was a no-brainer.

The piece finished with a call to action: "Fill out this contact form. That's all you need to do; we'll take it from there. This is a no cost consultation where we will review the situation, tell you how much it costs, and do the work for you."

That is typically what a blog article accomplishes. It gets your reader to make a decision to do something and then do it.

At this point, you might be asking: must all blog articles be designed to sell a product or service? Aren't there blog articles that simply present information?

Of course! There are many articles designed to simply present information to a reader. However, the same concepts still apply. You still want to grab your reader's attention, get them motivated to read the information, and keep them interested enough so they continue to the end.

TOPIC

You may already know the subject of your article. Occasionally, the subject just pops out thin air. For example, I often wake up in the middle of the night thinking, "Wow I need to write an article on blah, blah, blah." I keep a pad of paper next to my bed so I can record those ideas, no matter how silly. Some of my best ideas have come from those restless nights.

Sometimes a client might need me to write an article for them to fill out their blog and keep it active. In other words, I am simply required to give information to the people who visit their blog or website. The purpose of these articles is to help establish my clients as experts in their particular field and lend credibility to them.

On most cases, they want me to write an article that causes a percentage of their readers to make a purchase of their service or product. In other words, they need a copywriter.

A copywriter creates marketing or advertising copy. Their message tries to gain the interest of the reader and cause him or her to make a decision. Generally, this decision is to buy a product or service.

There are some decisions that you need to make before you start writing.

WHAT DO YOU WANT YOUR READER TO DO?

The first and most important question is, "What do you want the person who reads this to do?" You or your client may already have the answer to this question. They might have a product or service that they want people to buy. Perhaps all that's needed is for visitors to sign up for a newsletter, join a cause, or sign a petition.

In this type of article, you want your reader to make a decision. You may want them to buy your product, download a trial copy of the software, join a cause, or even take part in a discussion group.

The starting point for any article is determining what the reader's final decision should be. Everything word, picture, or video should lead the reader toward the outcome you desire. The title is designed to create enough interest that someone

Before you start

clicks on it. The next few paragraphs grab the reader's attention, demanding that they proceed forward. Everything that follows builds towards the outcome.

You need to know where you're aiming before you write a single word. It's the same as if you're shooting a bow and arrow at a target; if you don't know where the target is, you won't know where to aim or when you hit it.

Not only does identifying the desired outcome tell you what information you need to include in your article, but it also guides you in what to exclude. You can lose your reader very quickly by including information that has nothing to do with where you're going.

Once you know where you're headed, you can determine the primary phrases and words, known as keywords that you want to focus on in your article.

KEYWORDS

Search engines look through a document on the Internet and use complex sets of algorithms to figure out the meaning of the words. When you stop and think about it, it is actually a pretty amazing process.

Some robotic software reads your document and, based upon what it finds, determines the best way for people to locate it on the Internet. Keywords and phrases that someone would use if they were looking for that document are then determined.

Obviously, you want your document to be found by people who are using search engines. You can make it easier for these robots to determine what your document is about by cleverly including keywords and phrases in the title, headers, and text of the article.

You don't want to overdo it because the robot may then determine you're trying to fool it; this is known as search engine spamming. As you're designing and writing your document, sprinkle it with the key phrases and words that you want the search engine to pick up. Be sure the context in which they are included makes sense.

You can come up with keywords on your own, or you can use programs like the Google keyword tool to help you. There is a plethora of tools and services to aid you in this process. There are also a large number of articles, books, and courses available to train you on the methods and techniques.

Remember this key point as you perform this task and write your article. While you want the search engines to rank it as an easy to find, it is more important that human beings can read and understand what you've written. If you always keep the human being in mind and simply add a few hints for the search engines here and there, you can't go wrong.

OUTLINE

Now that you know what your article and have identified a few keywords, the next thing to do is create an outline. An outline is a plan; it summarizes the points your article will address. It also includes the order of the information to be presented.

The outline is especially important when you're writing a blog article for a client. Before you write a single word of the article,

Before you start

you need to create an outline and get your client's approval. The client's blessing creates an agreement between the two of you as to what you're going to write in your article.

You can make your outline as formal or informal as you wish. Of course, if you are creating one for your client, you should make sure it looks professional and present it on your company's letterhead. If no one's ever going to see it but you, whatever format you like is fine.

The main purpose of the outline is to organize your thoughts. By creating an outline before you write, you can prevent having to rewrite and revise over and over again. You can make sure you address everything you want and eliminate the information that is not needed.

An outline also helps you determine how your ideas and information connect to each other.

The method that I use to outline my articles is mind mapping. There are numerous mind mapping tools available. While some of them cost money, there are also several excellent free versions available.

A mind map basically presents an outline in graphic form. The main advantage is that it becomes very easy to see how things relate to each other; the order in which points will appear is easily determined through mind mapping. Most mind mapping software is available in an outline format suitable for most word processors.

My preferred product is called Freemind. It's very flexible, extremely fast, and works with most operating systems. With this product, you can create very complex diagrams. Additionally, there are numerous ways to connect the thoughts that you have recorded in your map.

Because I do much of my writing on a Google Chromebook®, I also use an application called MindMup. This handy tool accepts maps from Freemind and is usable directly from the Google Chrome® browser. This makes it easy for me to work on a mind map on my desktop, import it into MindMup, and then head out to the park or lunch to continue working.

Another purpose for the outline is to help identify areas of your article where you might need additional research or analysis. I include an image in my mind maps indicating areas where my knowledge is weak so I can create a list of what needs be researched later.

RESEARCH AND ANALYSIS

Unless you're an expert on the subject, you're almost certainly going to need to do a little research before you write your article. You should have a good idea of what research is needed from the exercise of outlining or mind mapping your work. It's generally a good idea to keep notes on areas that need further clarification as you are thinking up with your title, premise, keywords, and outline.

There are several purposes for your research. Obviously, you need to fill in the gaps in your knowledge. You can write an article about anything, even a subject about which you are totally ignorant, with the proper use of available research tools.

Before you start

Your research doesn't have to be time-consuming. If you have a thorough outline and mind map, you should have a tightly focused set of topics that need further study.

Avoid investigating areas that are not required to complete your article. Sometimes it's tempting to over research background information. Generally, there is no need to go to that much trouble. Remember, you only need enough data to allow you to write intelligently. You are not trying to become an expert on the subject.

A secondary purpose of performing research is to find documents by leading experts that you can reference in your article. This lends credibility to the information you present.

Set aside some time to do your research, locate the articles that you need, pull the information from them that's necessary, and then move on. Keep your goal of completing your blog article and publishing it on the Internet in mind.

The all-important title

Suppose you wrote the most wonderful, informative article the world has ever seen; something that explains one of the great secrets of the universe. You've created a wonderful essay that would improve the lives of everyone who read it.

Now throw that article out on the Internet, with tens of billions of other pages. Even with modern search engines and their extraordinary capability to index a plethora of information, it's difficult to make your article known to other people.

Assuming the search engines can even find your article, you have to get someone interested enough to want to look at it. You have the same problem with social media. You may post your article on Facebook®, but how do you convince people to want to read it?

They say you shouldn't judge a book by its cover, and you probably shouldn't judge the value of an article by its title. The fact of the matter is, sometimes the only thing a reader has available is the title. Given the vast amount of information that exists on the Internet today, your average person may only have a split second to make the decision whether or not to click on and read your post.

You could argue that the single most important thing about a blog article is its title. It doesn't matter how good the article is if no one ever reads it. Therefore, the title needs to grab your readers and pull them into the content. If it doesn't do that, you may find that few—if any—people read it at all.

The all-important title

On top of that, the words in the title are used by various search engines to define keywords by which people can find the article. The words in the title are often given added importance by search engine robots. After all, the title is the hook for getting someone to read your information.

WORKING TITLE

I don't even try and come up with my title before beginning to writing an article. When I start putting words on digital paper, I usually don't have a good idea of the hook that will draw people in. I've found that trying to figure out that hook before writing anything is a waste of time.

I do the same thing when I write a book. The working title is merely a placeholder that describes what I'm writing. It is not intended to be the hook. It is not sexy, and it never has anything to do with the final title of what I'm writing.

The point of coming up with the working title is simply to say, "This is what I'm writing about." If you're writing for a client, this gives you a name you can use in your discussions and emails about the article.

I find it important because it focuses my attention on the subject. I don't spend a lot of time on it, because it isn't going to survive for very long. By the time the article is finished and posted on the Internet, the working title will be changed to the actual title.

THE PROCESS

At some point while I'm writing an article, the title starts to become clear. Sometimes the perfect title just leaps out of the words or becomes obvious while I'm writing. On the other hand, I have occasionally spent hours banging my head on the wall while trying to think of the perfect hook to drag people into my article.

There are a number of things that go into the title of the article. You want it to resonate with people, so it's always a safe bet if a title is clever or funny. Clever is a good place to start, as people enjoy clever or humorous things.

You want to grab your reader by the shoulders and demand, "Get in here and read this!" If your title doesn't do that, you have failed.

Who is your reader? What is your target audience? What motivates them? What do those people want? What are they afraid of? The answers to these questions will help you figure out the title of your article.

Think about the subject of your article. Say your article was about the best ways to clean carpets. This is definitely not a sexy subject, so you need a good title to drag your reader inside. The title, "The Best Way to Clean Carpets," is not very exciting. How do you get your target audience motivated to read about the subject of the article?

THE HOOK

In most cases, your title has one purpose—to lure a reader inside your post. Sure, you might want to look sexy or be clever, but sexy or clever may not get someone to click and read your article.

The all-important title

Don't get me wrong; sometimes it's important to have a title that is poetic and imaginative. But often, a melodious title may not draw readers in like you would expect.

Begin with the hook, or the concept that gets your reader into the article. Why do they want to read an article about carpet cleaning, anyway?

One hook to employ is fear. Maybe they're afraid of allergies or the possibility of dirt carrying disease. Perhaps they believe dirty carpets breed cockroaches and invite rodents to live in a home. A title such as, "Prevent Infestations: 27 Cleaning Tips That Will Help," will speak to a reader who is motivated by fear.

You could also ask a question and then answer it. For example: "Tired of Cleaning Carpets? 27 Tips to Make It Easier."

Keep your titles short and concise. Search engines will truncate long titles, and people will stop reading them after a few words. I try and keep them between 50 and 72 characters.

SEARCH ENGINES

Another audience for your title is a search engine. Over the years, this has lessened in importance, but it still helps. Search engines will use keywords within your title to help index your article.

Keep in mind that your primary audience is people. Having keywords in your title may only add a small amount of importance for the purposes of indexing. Too many spammers in the past stuffed their titles with keywords to attempt to get their articles and websites to the top of the search engines.

If you can work a keyword or two into your title, it may help slightly with search engines, but if you can't make the title sound good to human beings then don't do it. It doesn't matter where you are in the rankings if no one wants to click the link.

Above the fold

The term "above the fold" comes from the old newspaper days. If you look at your newspaper as it sits in a newsstand, the part that you see facing up is referred to as above the fold. That's the most valuable real estate in the newspaper, as it's the first thing a reader is going to see.

Articles on the Internet work the same way. When someone clicks on a link to bring up your article, the first thing that the browser displays is the top of the article. This is the most important part of any article on the Internet—the digital version of above the fold.

Once someone clicks on the link to read your article, you have mere seconds to gain their attention. You have to put something of strong interest above the fold. The first paragraphs need to grab the reader and pull them straight into the rest of the text.

The entire purpose of the first couple of paragraphs is to get your readers excited enough to want to read everything else. Don't make it more complicated than that.

The first few paragraphs are a promise of something in return for their diligence in reading onward. One way you can do this is to ask a question or make a statement. Another tactic to employ is curiosity. Once they become curious, they keep reading.

Your article is educating your readers about something. You need to tell them there's a gap between what they know and

Above the fold

what you're going to tell them, and you need to do it as quickly as possible if you want them to spend time reading the rest of the article. For example, if you're writing about cleaning carpets, you could tell your reader that they're going to learn about a new technique that will save them time and impress their visitors.

Another important aspect to keep above the fold is an image. This first image is known as the featured image, and no blog article should be without one. This picture should be something that grabs their attention and reinforces the promise of your article. It should add value to your text.

Typically, the featured image should be on the right side and aligned with the top of the text in the article. Don't align images on the left; it tends to make reading the content more difficult.

Make the image about half the width of the page. This causes the text of your opening paragraphs appear thinner, which in turn makes your article more approachable and easier to read.

Put a caption on your image. When your reader sees the image, their eyes are automatically drawn to where the caption resides. Without a caption, your reader may abandon the article.

Sometimes you might want to put a video above the fold. This can be very successful, as it engages your reader right away. People like to watch videos, which makes them a good way to sell a product or service.

As you are designing and creating your blog article, keep in mind that the most vital thing you can do is to engage your reader from the start of your article. Everything you put above the fold should be both palatable and attention grabbing.

First section

Once you have completed the above the fold portion of your article, it's time to begin the first section. Put in a subheader to separate this content from the rest of your article.

The purpose of this first subheader is to give your reader a reason to move on to the next bit of content in your article. Tell them why they need to continue reading. What are they going to gain? What will be the reward if they continue into the next section?

Give your reader content focused on triggering emotion. Make them feel something. You've got plenty of time later to provide cold, hard facts, but right now you want to motivate them to continue reading. The best way to do that is to turn on an emotion or two.

These are called emotional triggers, and they are intended to do exactly what the phrase says. The emotional trigger causes the reader to feel emotions like anger, guilt, fear, and so forth.

A common tactic of political articles is to make the reader feel angry. They make the reader upset about something another politician has done or said. This prompts the reader to continue reading in order to find out what he or she can do about it.

Fear works well for some messages. I recently wrote a blog article about flood insurance that expanded on the fear of paying too much for unnecessary insurance.

First section

One of the best triggers is trust. Tell your reader that they can trust you, and tell them why. You might say you guarantee satisfaction, or you'll refund their money, no questions asked. That generates a high level of trust.

A trigger that's very common with charities and political advertisements is the feeling of being part of something. Many people want to belong. They feel good being one of the people who contributed to a cause or is part of an elite group.

Some people want to be at the head of the pack; they long to be the first one to do something or to see a new product. Those are the folks you see standing in line for the new smartphone. For some reason, they have to be the first person to see this newfangled device. You can appeal to that in your article.

For the carpet cleaning example we used earlier, you might use the emotional trigger of time. The carpet cleaning service might save somebody time cleaning the house. This frees them up to do other things with their life.

Of course, there's the old message of "keeping up with the Joneses." Lots of advertisements for gadgets use this particular emotional trigger. For example, you could prompt a reader to buy a new television by pointing out the fact that they don't want to be left behind with the same old piece of junk that everybody else has.

Connecting

The end of the first section is the perfect place to get your reader to help you spread the word about your article. You can do this by creating a way for them to tweet a message or graphic or share the information that they've just learned.

One effective method is to create a small graphic. This should be a colorful animation or a picture with a quote displayed on it. The website canva.com is perfect for creating these designer quotations.

Put a caption on the graphic that directs readers to tweet or share it. Many readers are willing to share messages with friends and followers. Of course, the message has to be something memorable to ensure that they'll want to share.

At the end of the first section, you can include a button to share the quote on Twitter or Facebook. You can embed graphics anywhere you want. In fact, you can even do more than one.

This allows your readers to help you spread the word about your article. You give them something that resonates with them—some kind of forceful and expressive quote—and they'll want to tell everyone they know about it.

This is how something becomes viral. Give your readers content they'll want share with others. If you take the time to make it easy for them to share, they will do so.

Connecting

If you're using WordPress for your blog, you'll be able to find plenty of plug-ins that support this action. I'm sure that other blogging platforms have similar functions.

By adding small graphics your reader can click or buttons they can push to share your content with their friends and colleagues, you can help readers spread your word. Often, they do this happily and totally without charge. Done properly, it's better than hiring an advertising agency.

The remaining sections

At the start of each of the remaining sections, include a subheader that tells people exactly what benefit they are going to get from the section. Use the subheader to promise them what they are going to learn in the content that follows.

If you can, include a keyword or key phrase in the subheader to reinforce your message to search engines. However, if doing so makes the subheader sound strange, it's best to avoid doing this. Above all else, your subheader should appeal to human beings.

Your first paragraph or two should tell your readers what they are going to get from the rest of section. Use action verbs, be bold, and tell them what's coming.

You can have as many sections as you want in your article. At a minimum, you should have at least two: the first section that gives the reader a reason to continue reading, and the second one that explains the topic in further detail.

One thing you can do is give people advice on how to put the product or service that you are selling to best use. You could make a "how to" section that can reinforce the value of your product or service.

Sprinkle in some quotes and testimonials describing the wonders of your product or service. Explain how the product or service has been beneficial to those who have used it. Forceful testimonials are always helpful, as they demonstrate that your product or service delivered on their promise.

The remaining sections

Include excerpts from interviews with satisfied customers in these remaining sections. Make sure they reinforce the message that your product or service is essential and will fulfill its promise.

It is a good idea to anticipate some of the questions that your readers (and hopefully clients) may have on their mind as they read. You can answer these questions in the text of your article.

For example, let's say you were selling a course about how to make money on eBay. Many of your readers might think that selling on eBay is difficult, so you could address that concern in your article. You might want to use a question and answer format and perhaps a few case studies as examples of successfully using your techniques.

Additionally, you can reinforce your message by including quotes from people who successfully made money on eBay. It might even be a good idea to include a video with snippets of interviews from people who have had great success.

Most articles will need at least one section in addition to the first two sections of the article. Create as many sections as you need to make your point, address obvious objections, and build interest in the product or service that you are offering.

The purpose of these additional sections is to give your readers motivation to purchase the product or service while addressing any objections they may have. You should build excitement while creating emotion and a sense of urgency in your readers. By the time they reach the end of your article, they should be practically demanding to purchase the product.

Final call to action

By the time your readers get to the end of your article, they should be foaming at the mouth and willing to do whatever you want them to do. It's time to spell out what they need to do in no uncertain terms.

Don't complicate this part of your article. Demand a clear and simple action from your reader. Don't confuse the issue by having more than one action. You want to give your reader one option and one action. For example, "Click the **Buy** button to start your course today."

Many times, you'll simply tell them to subscribe to your newsletter. This is a great way to end an informative article. By the time your reader gets here, they're hooked, have some affinity for you, and like your message. More than likely, they're going to go ahead and subscribe if you ask.

If you're selling a product or service, this is the point where you tell them to fill out the contact form, push the PayPal button, or whatever is appropriate for them to purchase the item.

A charity might request a donation or ask the reader to volunteer to help.

I've seen articles that ask readers to copy an image to their Facebook page or website. This image, which also includes a link, exposes other people to the information.

Final call to action

Spend a little time on this portion of your article. This is the culmination of all of your hard work and all of the previous sections. Their goal is for the reader to make a decision—preferably the one you want him to make—and to do it right now.

Images

Your article should include at least one image: the one that's above the fold, to the right of your opening paragraphs. The image should be pertinent to the subject at hand. The best images directly reinforce your message.

Ideally, sprinkle several images throughout your article. Images break up the text, making it easier to digest. They can also help engage your reader.

The main purpose of including images within your article is to keep your reader interested and committed to finishing the article. Most people get bored by long expanses of text, and you can prevent that with good images.

My blog articles tend to have anywhere from half a dozen to two dozen images scattered throughout the text. These images are intended to add value to the manuscript, as well as break it up so the reader isn't confronted with merely a wall of letters and numbers.

Do not include extraneous images that do not add value to the article. This tends to introduce the question of, "Why is this image here?" It confuses your reader and gives them a reason to leave the page.

Every image should have a caption that describes what that image means. A caption is a short bit of text—usually a sentence—that gives additional insight into the image. When a person is looking at an image on a website, their eyes

Images

automatically look for the caption. If the image doesn't have one, it can cause readers to abandon the article.

Be sure to include alt and title text with each image. Website software like WordPress has the built-in capability to include this text with every image in the media library.

These two attributes allow you to include a few additional keywords or phrases to your article. This is useful for search engines as they try and figure out which article is about. In addition, if the reader has images turned off, the alt text will be displayed, giving at least some context to an otherwise empty box on the screen.

The title attribute is displayed as tooltips, the pop-up bit of text that appears when your cursor hovers over an image. This is another way to add context to your images.

You can get images from a lot of different places. Of course, the most obvious way to get an image is to take pictures yourself. Since I'm a photographer, a lot of the images in my blogs are my own. Thus, I own the copyright, which means I can do whatever I want with it.

Depending on your budget, there are stock photo websites available. They generally have millions of different images. You are certain to find something to help your article in their vast store of photos and illustrations. The downside, of course, is that stock images can be very costly.

Fortunately, there are many free sources of images available. These include:

- ➢ Freeimages.com
- ➢ Gratisography.com
- ➢ Pixabay.com
- ➢ Pexels.com
- ➢ Picjumbo.com

Images on these sites are available for free and do not require attribution.

It is important to respect copyrights when selecting images. If you use images illegally, you could be sued and subject to paying damages. So make sure that the image you use is public domain or available without restriction under the Creative Commons license.

The Creative Commons license will tell you if the image may be used in a commercial environment. Many images are licensed for use for nonprofit or personal websites but not for purposes of monetary gain. Be sure to read the license under which the image is provided.

It is sometimes tempting to think that you can change the image as you wish. This is true if the image is public domain, or if this is allowed by the license. However, many images do not permit modifications, as per their licensing agreement.

Copyright also covers derivative works. You can't change an image and assume that you own the copyright on the modified image. The owner of the original image owns the copyright on any derivative images.

Images

The size of images is always a concern. I'm not referring to the dimensions of the image, but to its physical size in kilobytes or megabytes. The larger the image, the longer it takes to display on your readers' screens. Long display times can result in readers abandoning your page before they finish the article.

When you put images into your article, reduce the size so they load quickly. Be careful to not reduce the image size so much that it makes the image unattractive or unusable.

Be very cautious about including images depict motion. These kinds of images can take a long time to load, and unless they add quite a bit of value to your article I would tend to avoid them.

Some image formats cause the image to slowly appear as they are loaded. The GIF format, which is a very old method for encoding a picture, has that capability. I would recommend avoiding the use of this kind of technology. In my opinion, it makes a web page look tacky and unprofessional.

Audio and Video

You can include the audio for an interview or description within your article. WordPress plug-ins allow you to embed audio tracks on a page. This can be a very powerful way to add details without weighing down your article with excessive text.

Video is an even more powerful way to add value to your blog article. Embedding short clips can illustrate points. You can even include whole interviews to add context to your writing.

I like to include videos because they add a lot of information outside of the flow of text. Thus, readers are not slowed down by even more words and can view the video if they want more information.

In addition to adding value for your readers, another major reason to include videos is that YouTube indexes them. This is a totally different way for readers to find your blog.

Do not embed your videos in such a way that they automatically play as soon as the page loads. That's extremely annoying, especially on tablets and smartphones. Let your readers decide if they want to view the video. Personally, if I open up a web page that automatically plays a video, I will immediately leave the page.

Today, it's quite common to create reasonably high-quality videos using a smartphone. This kind of footage tends to be shaky. Nonetheless, a smartphone will work just fine to create a video in a pinch

Audio and Video

For a more professional recording experience, you can purchase inexpensive video cameras from many stores and online retailers. I've seen high-quality video cameras going for under $50.

Most digital cameras include an option to create video. In fact, I think it's difficult to find a digital camera today that doesn't include video. These can produce excellent quality footage that is more than adequate for use in a blog article.

If your budget allows, you can use high-end, professional quality video equipment. You can purchase your own equipment, you can rent the equipment from many different shops, or you can rent a studio along that comes with the equipment that you need. You can also hire a person to make the videos for you.

The most important thing to remember when you create a video is make sure the lighting is good. An otherwise perfect video can easily be ruined if the lighting is not correct. It should neither be too bright nor too dim. The subject of lighting in video could take up a whole book on its own.

Another important part of a video is quality audio. It doesn't necessarily need to be stereo, but it needs to sound clean and lack any hissing or noise. As with lighting, bad audio can ruin an otherwise perfect video.

Ideally, you should be able to shoot your video so it is ready to put up on the web with little or no editing. This can save you a lot of work.

Many people put their videos up on YouTube, and that's perfectly acceptable. The main advantage of YouTube, of course, is that it's free. YouTube has many tools that allow you to edit your videos directly online. You can take advantage of these to do some minor fix-ups without taking lots of time.

There are many other sites where you can store and stream your videos. Many of them cost money, but they have advantages over YouTube. For me, the main advantage of using a paid streaming site such as Vimeo is that there are no advertisements.

Once you've made a lot of your own videos, you might find it useful to purchase video editing software. There are many different applications that allow you to perform magic on your videos. They can be priced anywhere from $75 to upwards of $1,000.

Video is a great way to add value for your readers. By strategically including clips in your article, you can keep your readers engaged and interested.

Conclusion

You can write an article for a blog that causes a high percentage of the people who read it to make a purchase, sign up for a newsletter, click a link, or join a cause. The techniques that are outlined in this book can help you with that goal.

One of the interesting things about copywriting is you don't necessarily have to be a good writer. Instead, you need to be a good persuader.

The concept of this kind of article is very straightforward. You create a title that gets the attention of someone as they scan search engine results, a link on a website, or read an email. The title begs to be clicked.

Once a person has clicked on the title and is looking at your article, the next task is to get them excited. You have a matter of seconds to convince them to stay and read the rest of your material. You can do that with a paragraph or two of text, a good picture placed to the right, and perhaps a video.

Once your reader has gotten past the above the fold area, your next task is to cause them to feel some emotion. You want to pull their emotional trigger with something that makes them excited, fearful, angry, jealous, guilty, and so forth. This causes them to want to move forward and read the rest of your material.

After that, you can handle any objections, as well as reinforce your message with testimonials, interviews, examples, and

Conclusion

whatever else you need to bring your product or service to life for your reader. Use as many sections as needed.

Finally, you come to the point where you want them to press the buy button, subscribe to the newsletter, join the discussion, or do whatever it is you set out for them to do. The best way to do this is to tell them to do it.

If you successfully wrote an article using these techniques, people will be pulled from the beginning, stay until the end, and ultimately do what you want them to do.

This book has provided a description of one method of using copywriting to create an article for blog that produces results. There is much more to the art of copywriting than this. I hope this has been a good start for you and will help you on your journey to sell your product, service, or whatever else you are trying to do.

Before you go

If you scroll to the last page in this eBook, you will have the opportunity to leave feedback and share the book with Before You Go. I'd be grateful if you turned to the last page and shared the book.

Also, if you have time, please leave a review. Positive reviews are incredibly useful. If you didn't like the book, please email me at rich@thewritingking.com and I'd be happy to get your input.

TAKE CONTROL OF YOUR PERSONAL BRAND ON LINKEDIN

An Interview with Richard G Lowe Jr, Senior Branding Expert and Bestselling Author of Focus on LinkedIn

Richard G Lowe Jr

Learn how to use LinkedIn to get more and better qualified leads

Click the link for your free eBook and to sign up for tips

linkedin.thewritingking.com

linkedin.thewritingking.com

About the Author

Follow me on Twitter: @richardlowejr

Richard Lowe has leveraged more than 35 years of experience as a Senior Computer Manager and Designer at four companies into that of a bestselling author, blogger, ghostwriter, and public speaker. He has written hundreds of articles for blogs and ghostwritten more than a dozen books and has published manuscripts about computers, the Internet, surviving disasters, management, and human rights. He is currently working on a ten-volume science fiction series – the Peacekeeper Series – to be published at the rate of three volumes per year, beginning in 2016.

Richard started in the field of Information Technology, first as the Vice President of Consulting at Software Techniques, Inc. Because he craved action, after six years he moved on to work for two companies at the same time: he was the Vice President of Consulting at Beck Computer Systems and the Senior Designer at BIF Accutel. In January 1994, Richard found a home at Trader Joe's as the Director of Technical Services and Computer Operations. He remained with that incredible company for almost 20 years before taking an early retirement to begin a new life as a professional writer. He is currently the CEO of The Writing King, a company that provides all forms of writing services, the owner of The EBay King, and a Senior Branding Expert for LinkedIn Makeover. You can find a current list of all books on his Author Page and

About the Author

take a look at his exclusive line of coloring books at The Coloring King.

Richard has a quirky sense of humor and has found that life is full of joy and wonder. As he puts it, "This little ball of rock, mud, and water we call Earth is an incredible place, with many secrets to discover. Beings fill our corner of the universe, and some are happy, and others are sad, but each has their unique story to tell."

His philosophy is to take life with a light heart, and he approaches each day as a new source of happiness. Evil is ignored, discarded, or defeated; good is helped, enriched, and fulfilled. One of his primary interests is to educate people about their human rights and assist them to learn how to be happy in life.

Richard spent many happy days hiking in national parks, crawling over boulders, and peering at Indian pictographs. He toured the Channel Islands off Santa Barbara and stared in fascination at wasps building their homes in Anza-Borrego. One of his joys is photography, and he has photographed more than 1,200 belly dancing events, as well as dozens of Renaissance fairs all over the country.

Because writing is his passion, Richard remains incredibly creative and prolific; each day he writes between 5,000 and 10,000 words, diligently using language to bring life to the world so that others may learn and be entertained.

Richard is the CEO of The Writing King, which specializes in fulfilling any writing need. You can find out more at https://www.thewritingking.com/, and emails are welcome at rich@thewritingking.com

Books by Richard G Lowe Jr.

Business Professional Series

On the Professional Code of Ethics and Business Conduct in the Workplace – Professional Ethics: 100 Tips to Improve Your Professional Life - have you ever wondered what it takes to be successful in the professional world? This book gives you some tips that will improve your job and your career.

Help! My Boss is Whacko! - How to Deal with a Hostile Work Environment - sometimes the problem is the boss. There are all kinds of managers, some competent, some incompetent, and others just plain whacked. This book will help you understand and handle those different types of managers.

Help! I've Lost My Job: Tips on What to do When You're Unexpectedly Unemployed – suddenly having to leave your job can be a harsh and emotional time in your life. Learn some of the things that you need to consider and handle if this happens to you.

Help! My Job Sucks Insider Tips on Making Your Job More Satisfying and Improving Your Career – sometimes conditions conspire to make the regular trek to a job feel like a trip through Dante's Inferno. Sometimes, these are out of our control, such as a malicious manager or incompetent colleague. On the other hand, we can take control of our lives and workplace and improve our situation. Get this book to learn what you can do when your job sucks.

Books by Richard G Lowe Jr.

How to Manage a Consulting Project: Make money, get your project done on time, and get referred again and again – I found that being a consultant is a great way to earn a living. Managing a consulting project can be a challenge. This book contains some tips to help you so you can deliver a better product or service to your customers.

How to be a Good Manager and Supervisor, and How to Delegate – Lessons Learned from the Trenches: Insider Secrets for Managers and Supervisors – I've been a manager for over thirty years I learned many things about how to get the job done and deliver quality service. The information in this book will help you manage your projects to a high level of quality.

Focus on LinkedIn – Learn how to create a LinkedIn profile and to network effectively using the #1 business social media site.

Home Computer Security Series

Safe Computing is Like Safe Sex: You have to practice it to avoid infection – Security expert and Computer Executive, Richard Lowe, presents the simple steps you can take to protect your computer, photos and information from evil doers and viruses. Using easy-to-understand examples and simple explanations, Lowe explains why hackers want your system, what they do with your information, and what you can do to keep them at bay. Lowe answers the question: how to you keep yourself say in the wild west of the internet.

Books by Richard G Lowe Jr.

Disaster Preparation and Survival Series

<u>Real World Survival Tips and Survival Guide: Preparing for and Surviving Disasters with Survival Skills</u> – CERT (Civilian Emergency Response Team) trained and Disaster Recovery Specialist, Richard Lowe, lays out how to make you, your family, and your friends ready for any disaster, large or small. Based upon specialized training, interviews with experts and personal experience, Lowe answers the big question: what is the secret to improving the odds of survival even after a big disaster?

<u>Creating a Bug Out Bag to Save Your Life: What you need to pack for emergency evacuations</u> - When you are ordered to evacuate—or leave of your free will—you probably won't have a lot of time to gather your belongings and the things you'll need. You may have just a few minutes to get out of your home. The best preparation for evacuation is to create what is called a bug out bag. These are also known as go-bags, as in, "grab it and go!"

Professional Freelance Writer Series

<u>How to Operate a Freelance Writing Business, and How to be a Ghostwriter – Proven Tips and Tricks Every Author Needs to Know about Freelance Writing: Insider Secrets from a Professional Ghostwriter</u> – This book explains how to be a ghostwriter, and gives tips on everything from finding customers to creating a statement of work to delivering your final product.

<u>How to Write a Blog That Sells and How to Make Money From Blogging: Insider Secrets from a Professional Blogger:</u>

Books by Richard G Lowe Jr.

<u>Proven Tips and Tricks Every Blogger Needs to Know to Make Money</u> – There is an art to writing an article that prompts the reader to make a decision to do something. That's the narrow focus of this book. You will learn how to create an article that gets a reader interested, entices them, informs them, and causes them to make a decision when they reach the end.

Other Books by Richard Lowe Jr

How to Be Friends with Women: How to Surround Yourself with Beautiful Women without Being Sleazy – I am a photographer and frequently find myself surrounded by some of the most beautiful women in the world. This book explains how men can attract women and keep them as friends, which can often lead to real, fulfilling relationships.

How to Throw Parties like a Professional: Tips to Help You Succeed with Putting on a Party Event – Many of us have put on parties, and I know it can be a daunting and confusing experience. In this book, I share what I learned from hosting small house parties to shows and events.

Additional Resources

Is your career important to you? Find out how to move your career in any direction you desire, improve your long-term livelihood, and be prepared for any eventuality. Visit the page below to sign up to receive valuable tips via email, and to get a free eBook about how to optimize your LinkedIn profile.

http://list.thewritingking.com/

I've written and published many books on a variety of subjects. They are all listed on the following page.

https://www.thewritingking.com/books/

On that site, I also publish articles about business, writing, and other subjects. You can visit by clicking the following link:

https://www.thewritingking.com

To find out more about me or my photography, you can visit these sites:

Personal website: https://www.richardlowe.com
Photography: http://www.richardlowejr.com
LinkedIn Profile: https://www.linkedin.com/in/richardlowejr
Twitter: https://twitter.com/richardlowejr

If you have any comments about this book, feel free to email me at rich@thewritingking.com

Premium Writing Services

Do you have a story that needs to be told? Have you been trying to write a book for ages but never can seem to find the time to get it done? Do you want to brand your business, but don't know how to get started?

The Writing King has the answer. We can help you with any of your writing needs.

Ghostwriting. We can write your book, which entails interviewing you to get your story, writing the book and then working with you to revise it until complete. To discuss your book, contact The Writing King today.

Website Copy. Many businesses include the text on their sites as an afterthought, and that can result in lost sales and leads. Hire The Writing King to review your site and recommend changes to the text which will help communicate your message and improve your sales.

Blogging. Build engagement with your customers by hiring us to write a weekly or semi-weekly article for your blog, LinkedIn or other social media. Contact The Writing King today to discuss your blogging needs.

LinkedIn. LinkedIn is of the most important vehicles for finding new business, and a professionally written profile works to pulling in those leads. Write or update your profile today.

Technical Writing. We have broad experience in the computer, warehousing and retail industries, and have

Premium Writing Services

written hundreds of technical documents. Contact The Writing King today to find out how we can help you with your technical writing project.

The Writing King has the skills and knowledge to help you with any of your writing needs. Call us today to discuss how we can help you.

www.ingramcontent.com/pod-product-compliance
Lightning Source LLC
Chambersburg PA
CBHW071515210326
41597CB00018B/2766